Heart and Soul in the Boardroom

Heart and Soul in the Boardroom

Heart and Soul in the Boardroom

Robert L. Cooper

Contact Information:
RL Cooper Associates
24 Greenwood Drive
New City, NY 10956
(845) 639-1741
info@rlcooperassoc.com
www.rlcooperassoc.com

This book was printed in the United States of America.

To order additional copies of this book, contact:
Xlibris Corporation
1-888-795-4274
www.Xlibris.com
Orders@Xlibris.com
72622

Contents

Acknowledgments...7

Preface...9

Pulse Point 1:   Why Having Heart Is So Important 11

Pulse Point 2:   Formulas for Producing Profitability.......................17

Pulse Point 3:   There Can Be No True Promotion without the Heart....23

Pulse Point 4:   Let Light Shine on Your Heart 29

Pulse Point 5:   Applying the Lessons of the Heart............................35

Conclusion 39

Appendix: A True Story of Heart and Soul in the Boardroom 41

Testimonials 44

Acknowledgments

Acknowledgments

Thank you, Peter Lorenzo, for your friendship and for living the principles in this book every day. Thank you, Tony Fedina, for your input and friendship—you are another professional who embodies these principles. Thank you, John Fontana, for recognizing why this book's message is so important for business students and the future success of our organizations. Thank you, Jack Steiman and Yolanda Dandridge, for your commitment to spiritual evolution and your belief in this book's message.

Thank you, Anne Tarpey, Catherine Lopez, and Gwen Faust, for being such good friends and individuals who exhibit the highest standards of integrity—people of true heart.

Thank you, Dr. Deepak Chopra, for being my inspiration. Your wonderful book *Creating Affluence* has become a lifelong companion.

Most of all, I want to thank my wife, Debbie, and son, Gordon. You both make my heart feel a sense of happiness and gratitude—I love you both very much.

Preface

Preface

I had the privilege to attend an inspirational seminar given by Dr. Wayne Dyer. Dr. Dyer was speaking about the contrast between the "morning and afternoon" of one's life. According to Dyer, the morning refers to the period of "accumulation"; the afternoon is the period of our lives that is all about "meaning." The afternoon involves one's spiritual evolution and living a life of complete and total integrity. I approached the Dyer seminar with the principles of the book before you now on my mind. However, I had not yet selected a title. As Dr. Dyer was speaking, the title popped into my head. I felt it with such clarity that I could not wait to write it down.

During a break, I went to speak with Dr. Dyer. I thought that actually speaking to him would be impossible since the line was so long. Then all of a sudden, the line became a circle. I moved toward the front of the circle and then found myself in the middle of the circle, just Dr. Dyer and me. I said, "Wayne, how do I get my new book to you?" He replied, "Is it already written?" I said, "No, but I had a title." He said, "What is it?" My response was "Heart and Soul in the Boardroom." He asked me when did I arrive at the title. I explained that it came to me while he was speaking about the afternoon of our life. He said, "I love the title, send it to Hay House, they will get it to me."

As I write this book, I know that I was destined to speak with Dr. Dyer. He inspires me because of his authenticity—he speaks from his heart.

Heart and Soul in the Boardroom is written for current and future leaders and for any leader aspiring to make a difference in the lives of others. This book is about inspiring passion, compassion, and spirit in the workplace. With these principles, one can create and sustain work environments where peace and integrity are found within the fabric of the organizational culture. There must, however, be a willingness to change some of the rules of the game. Leaders must be held accountable to lead their organizations as if the leader is in the afternoon of his or her life. This means that compassion, kindness, and honesty come before bonuses. This means that success is more than just profitability in the economic sense. Success is about making a difference for other people and allowing employees to feel that they are contributing and are making a difference.

It is recommended that this book be read cover to cover. Then read Pulse Point 5 every day. By simply becoming more aware and focusing on the heart lessons, work environments will begin to become places of happiness, contentment, and success.

I felt guided to write this book. It is in absolute alignment with my core purpose, which is to empower individuals and groups to reach their full potential in their professional environments as well as in life. My sincere hope in writing this book is that it will be a catalyst for changing the way business success is defined. As the definition changes, behaviors will change. As behaviors change, business outcomes will change for the betterment of all. The intent behind this book is to mobilize a new mindset that will prevent us from ever seeing another Enron collapse—an attack of an organizational heart that was deadly. Instead, boardrooms across the world will begin to beat with a heart and a new vibrancy.

Robert L. Cooper

Pulse Point 1

Pulse Point 1

Why Having Heart Is So Important

If only I had a dollar for every time I hear a leader say, "No margin, no mission." This cliché is used far too cavalierly as if others just don't understand what it means to be profitable. The problem that I have is that unfortunately, many of the people speaking these words are really saying, "No margin, there goes my bonus." Their concern is not at all whether the security guard, receptionist, or accountant is satisfied with their work. In fact, they have little regard at all about their employees' 401(k) plans. They are not worried about the development of their people. Sure, they might stand up in front of their employees and say, "Our people are our most important asset." The question is, how many boardroom executives really mean it? My experience says, there are several who do but not nearly enough.

Heart is, and always has been, critically important. Every time someone goes home with high blood pressure because their boss was insensitive, *it is important*. Anytime an executive is still smiling when getting into his or her limousine or company car while hundreds of people are being laid off, *it is important*. Anytime an executive tells Wall Street that their company is doing well as the books are being manipulated to reflect that claim, *it is important*. Anytime an employee dies and a leader is more interested in a lunch appointment than paying respect, *it is important*. Anytime an executive thinks that finishing a report is a higher priority than a child's graduation, *it is important*. Anytime everyone in the organization is expected to focus solely on work at the expense of their personal lives, *it is important*.

Are people expected to start living only after they retire? Who said business is a game and not a part of life? We bring our whole selves to the workplace. The reality is that we are all spiritual beings dressed up as businesspeople, not the other way around. Unfortunately, so many of us have lost our souls. We replaced kindness and compassion with spreadsheets and Dunkin' Donuts coffee. I love the coffee; it's the sugar that's often missing.

Let me be very clear about something. I am a spiritual businessman. I do understand that in order to grow, our businesses need to be profitable. What I am challenging here is the thinking of many business leaders that act as if heart and soul in the boardroom is not important. You notice I said *act*, not *say*. Many businesspeople are quite gifted at giving speeches about how much they care. The question is, who is the speechwriter? Is it someone who knows how to make things look a certain way, or is it a person who is genuinely acting with heart? A person with heart knows that they are on this earth to serve others. A person with heart vibrates with a pure frequency filled with compassion and kindness. A person with heart never has to think twice about what they say because they come from a place of integrity. A person with heart does not hide behind PowerPoint slides. A person with heart is transparent. A person with heart exposes their heart, and everyone around them feels its beat as a life-form that propels the organizations profitability.

My feeling is, leaders that are insensitive to their employees and misrepresent the truth to shareholders deserve to be locked away in cells so they can have plenty of time to think and reflect. It's not punishment that we should seek; it's reflection.

We need to learn to forgive those among us that lost their heart along the way. We all know that they had hearts when they were born. We are all beautiful spiritual beings. Unfortunately, egos often cause us to lose our way. This does not mean that someone is a bad person. We must learn *not* to judge. It means that we either have not entered into or we are not in tuned to the afternoon of our life—our ability to look inside and come to terms with how we lost feeling and compassion for others.

The truth is that when you look at a baby, all you see is pure joy. They give love and are so innocent. They are well-intentioned spiritual beings. As the years go by, many people lose their innocence and their hearts. They don't want to lose it; ego gets in the way. The ego says that if a person accumulates many possessions, they are successful. The ego says that if you look a certain way, you are beautiful. The reality is, we are all one. The president of a corporation is no different from a receptionist. They are both one, not separated because of their titles.

Unfortunately, the business landscape is filled with ego judgments. If you hold a certain position, you may be viewed as valuable or essential. If you hold another position, you may be viewed as not important or nonessential. The mere fact that we allow these judgments to exist means that the heart has been lost. Possessing a heart means we understand that all of us are connected—that we are one and that we are all important. We need to replace judgment with compassion and kindness. We should seek to understand everyone that we come in contact with.

"Having heart" is important, and it all begins with respect. First, we must have self-respect. True self-respect means that the minute we stop caring for other's needs, we should stop and reflect. In this reflection, we will find our truth. This becomes an opportunity to replace greed with understanding and to forego personal gain with service to others. Self-respect implies a connection with your true meaning and the "afternoon" of your life. You start to recognize that living a *life of meaning* can be and is pure bliss.

I can't help but think of the images of CEOs that have been convicted of inflicting pain on the organizations they served. I recently watched an interview with an incarcerated former CEO. When I closed my eyes, I saw a broken soul. This individual, through reflection, now understands that he allowed his ego to deceive him. He may have begun the journey of

13

coming to the truth. Although he outwardly claimed innocence, the inward journey is what really matters most. I believe that through reflection he came to understand the need to live the rest of his life by moving into the afternoon of his life, finding true meaning. Maybe it means that one day he will write a book that will inspire other business leaders to do the same. Perhaps he will share his insights with others in jail and help to transform their thinking. Perhaps then other leaders who have lost their way will find some sense of inner peace.

A heart lost can be transformed into a heart found. We can all learn to be compassionate again. We can all learn to respect everyone as an equal soul again. We can all find ourselves again. In this journey called life, we come to many crossroads. If we always choose to move toward living in the afternoon of our lives—toward true meaning—we will leave this earth a better place. It's important that we do not delineate between work and play but do both with meaning.

The fact that you put on a business suit does not mean that you left yourself behind. The many e-mails and meetings that you have to deal with are realities of business, not reasons to lose your heart. You can choose to deal with other people's egos by maintaining your own sense of inner peace and integrity. You may encounter all sorts of negative energy. Your response should *always* be from a place of heart. When you respond from that place, you bring your energy to a level of total compassion and understanding. This will often lift the other person's energy to a place where you can both really see and understand each other. Never allow someone else's lost heart cause you to lose yours. To the contrary, show your heart at all times. You become the model of an authentic heart. We can transcend the business playing field by raising our energy to the beat of a kind and compassionate heart. Never sell your soul to the self-serving ego-minded suits. If you do, you will pay a tremendous price. You will stay in the morning of your life—accumulating things yet never finding true and lasting meaning. You will walk around smiling, but your soul will be crying. Enlightened souls that you encounter will see right through you. They will not want to do business with you, and eventually, your career and your life will derail. You will leave this earth as someone that served him or herself, yet your spiritual bank will be totally empty. This is the greatest loss of all. You will not be able to truly rest in peace. True peace means serving the needs of others. This means you understand that hurting others is not living a life of meaning. To live a life of meaning, you must keep your awareness high so that you see life on a multidimensional level. You see yourself, and you see everyone else at the same time.

You must always think cause and effect. Let's look at a very basic example. Think about the boss who asks his assistant to get him a cup of coffee every morning but never reciprocates. Translation: "I am the boss, you are here to serve me." A person who understands the law of service would want to serve the other person as well from time to time. The title one holds is absolutely irrelevant. We are all equal souls. When you hold the door open for someone, do you ask what is your title? We must all learn to care and respect everyone. If you provide service based on the ego, you are living in the morning of your life. You will gain the reputation as someone that leads with ego, with the belief that you will only serve someone else if you have something to gain from the interaction.

Leading with a heart translates into having sincere and loyal followers. The key word is *sincerity*. People will only sincerely follow if they know you care. They want to know that you have a heart. They want to know that their needs matter. Great business leaders are no different from great people. The fact that they are wearing a suit and sit in the boardroom is irrelevant. We need to understand that to have organizations that mean something and are sustainable, we must have heart in every corner of the workplace—it is essential that it begin in boardrooms.

"Having heart" always means something and is always important!

Pulse Point 2

Pulse Point 2

Formulas for Producing Profitability

Performance Plus Heart

It is difficult for any business to survive without making a profit. However, profits generated without the heart means that no true profit has actually been made. Many of you may be thinking, profits are profits, period. What does profitability really mean? Most people define profitability as the remainder left over after all expenses have been paid.

In actuality, profitability is not defined strictly in material terms. You can't see true profitability on a spreadsheet. You cannot judge profitability by an executive driving a fancy sports car around bonus time. True profitability exists when there is evidence of heart in the boardroom and throughout the organization. Indicators of whether the heart is present are determined by some basic questions about how an organization performs:

✓ Do people inside the organization know that they are valued?
✓ Do employees know they are respected?

✓ Do tears flow because supervisors treat staff members poorly, or is positive, constructive criticism the organizational practice?

✓ Are people's spirits broken, or are souls encouraged to soar?

Compassion Plus Integrity Equals Profitability

I believe that with compassion and integrity, an organization, and ultimately the world, can be profitable. Compassion is felt in the heart. People should always show compassion and true understanding for one another. Displaying compassion means giving hope. People thrive in environments where compassion is found throughout their everyday existence. Some of you may be wondering, "What does compassion have to do with profitability?" The answer is everything!

If we can replace greed with compassion, condescending viewpoints with compassion, sarcasm with compassion, competition with compassion, arrogance with compassion, we can achieve just about anything. What holds people back from reaching their full potential is the belief that individuals are just objects to achieve a means—profitability. People are not objects; they are real. They are human beings that are full of emotion. They are full of dreams. They want to ignite their passions. Giving compassion means letting others know that they are valued. A person's spirituality, their soul, is not like a coat that is left outside the door when they walk into the workplace. They should not be expected to check their heart at the door. Unfortunately, many organizations say their employees are their most important asset but behave as if their hearts should be checked at the door or locked up in their desk. In a healthy, profitable organization, every person's heart should be alive and pulsating so that profits will flow throughout the veins of the organization. The heart pumps blood that makes the whole system work. When even one vein is clogged, the heart is compromised and begins to shut down. When the heart shuts down, by definition, the system is dead. If the system is dead, how can it be profitable?

It is the health of people's souls that determine the final profitability score. The only score that truly matters is how much compassion is brought to the boardroom table. You must be able to feel the organizational pulse which is measured by compassion for others. Without it, the organization's heart becomes strained.

Without compassion, you are playing a losing game. You are not inspiring trust, kindness, peace, and passion. You are part of the problem and can't possibly see the solution. Without compassion, you are going on a trip without a map. You are lost, and unless you recapture compassion, you will not be found. You can't be found. How can you expect to be found unless you recapture your heart?

The other ingredient of a healthy organization is integrity. Any workplace that is absent of integrity, absolutely, positively cannot be considered profitable. I understand Wall Street is only concerned with the bottom-line numbers. Revenue growth and margin expansion are but a few of the terms thrown about by the Wall Street gurus. However, these terms do not matter without integrity present within the fabric of the organization. Integrity is the web woven between an individual and his/her soul.

You might think that it is all about perception, but it's really all about spiritual reality and integrity. You can try to fool yourself, but your soul knows the truth. Integrity does not mean you have to be perfect—no one is. Integrity simply means being truthful with yourself and others. Your heart knows the truth. So ask yourself, "Do I listen to my heart? Do I ignore the signals that point me toward my truth? Do I play to please others or to satisfy my true spiritual core, the essence of what makes me who I am?"

We all came into this world as compassionate human beings. Just spend a few minutes with babies and look at their joy, feel their love. They are pure love and pure integrity. All they know is beauty. Everything they see is to be observed, not judged. Everyone is equal. If you give them love, you will receive all the love you would ever want or need. Their spirits are alive. They are pure potential, and they are pure joy.

Spend some time in nature. Just look at all the beauty. Nature is so real, so alive. We are on this earth for a short time, but the oceans are for eternity. The more you experience the pure joy in nature, think about how your heart feels. That feeling could be present in every aspect of your life. You can feel this feeling and give it to everyone you meet. You can give this to your family, friends, coworkers, and every person you see every day. It all becomes real when you connect with your truth.

Your truth is your heart pulsating with compassion. Your truth is your heart beating with beauty. Your truth is allowing the person you were when you were born to come alive. In a sense, we all need to be reborn. The minute we turn our attention away from kindness and compassion and focus on deception, lies, and manipulation, we have poisoned our environment. We need to replace fear with compassion. We need to live a life of complete and total integrity. Living a life of integrity will set you free. You will be truly profitable.

Profits flow when you are connecting with your truth. You are that baby being reborn; your soul has a chance to come alive. If your soul has died, you have died. You might be breathing, but without integrity, you may as well be dead. The absence of integrity means you are not living fully. You have robbed our planet of beauty and kindness. You have contributed to the pain and suffering of others, including your own.

This chapter is all about the concept of developing a spiritual formula for winning. I believe that the only way you win is to live a life of total compassion for others and integrity. Winning means that you have enriched our planet through your desire to serve others from a place of complete integrity. We lose the minute we lose sight of the lessons we brought into this lifetime. The minute we stop giving to others, we lose. When we judge others, we lose. If we don't see the beauty in others, we lose.

So we call on you to make adjustments and reinstate compassion and integrity. Replace greed with compassion. Replace sarcasm with respect. Replace emptiness with wholeness. We all have the capacity to be part of the solution. We must bring our spiritual awareness to the workplace in order to see the truth. By doing so, we elevate ourselves above the game board and go to a higher plane where it is easier to see solutions. It's from this perspective that we can see the truth. If you look down at the board and see yourself and others not living the truth, come back and create the truth. You should help others by modeling truth and integrity for all to observe.

Challenge yourself to become a teacher of goodwill and a symbol of the heart. If you are not being open and honest, become open and honest. If you are criticizing and judging others, instead, learn to listen and understand. If you are not treating everyone equally and with respect, commit to giving total respect to all. If you are not being kind, experience increased profitability by giving kindness. Replace ugliness with beauty. If you see someone not reaching their potential, do everything possible to help them reach their full potential.

True profitability flows when you have inner peace. This peacefulness comes from knowing that all of your giving comes from your heart. Your heart beats and pulsates to the drum of integrity. When integrity is the life force that flows through your veins, you feel such a sense of calmness because compassion and kindness is life's greatest gift; it fills your heart with joy. Having a heart and living with a heart means that no matter what happens to you for the rest of your life, you will be truly blessed. This is the true meaning of success.

You are successful when your mere presence brings joy to everyone that comes in contact with you. Your kindness and compassion brings healing to others. They feel your kindness and find strength in your compassion. You never need to tell others about your accomplishments. You only need to be you. Your sense of self is so pure and so intact that everyone wants to be in your space. You don't need people to tell you about how much they value you; you only need to know that your kindness is a gift to the world.

Profitability can be found through the hearts and mind of others. Just look into their eyes and feel their appreciation. You can sense the difference you have made by serving their needs. You form a true bond through your integrity. You feel such a sense of peace by seeing their smile. Work feels easy and effortless because you are giving to others and they in turn give back to you. The more you give, the more you receive. The more others give, the more profitable you become. Your coworkers become your greatest supporters. They are willing to go the extra mile to see you succeed. They want you to be successful because they care about you as a person. They respect you and want the best for you. This makes you feel like you are swimming downstream, not fighting the tide. Everything becomes easier and effortless as a result of your gentle heart. You feel profitable all the time. You feel a sense of happiness and joy, a feeling of inner peace. Never compromise your integrity, and you will feel profitable all the time.

Pulse Point 3

There Can Be No True Promotion without the Heart

W hen you are absent of heart, you do not belong on the organizational chart. Your name may be on the chart, but your soul is gone. You might move up the hierarchy and believe you have been promoted, but it has not been earned. Enlightened souls within the organization know you are not deserving of the position you hold. Yes, your name shows up, but you are not real in the eyes of others.

Many people reading this are saying, "Come on, I am a vice president. What do you mean?" What we mean here is that a vice president without a heart may well exist physically but is not viewed as a fully functioning, positive energy within the organization and therefore does not really exist. Sure, we can see the body, but that's it. No one *wants* to be in your presence, except for others with lost hearts too. Those who report to you as subordinates do what they are told as a requirement to keep their own position within the organization. There is no sense of true camaraderie or teamwork.

The truth is, the minute an enlightened soul is in a position of power, you will be "officially" gone. You see, your darkness will be exposed by the light force of others. It will become apparent that you were never really listened to or heard by others because you did not really care about others. Your ego was getting the best of you. You felt that you were superior to others. You believed that nothing good could happen without your involvement. You were always wrong with your assumptions. In the eyes of others, you were not respected or regarded as "real." Without a compassionate heart, you were, in effect, lifeless and viewed as an obstacle by enlightened coworkers.

The only way a promotion becomes meaningful is when others *want* to follow. If the "want" is not there, the promotion is not truly real. People want and are motivated to follow someone that brings joy to their lives and compassion to the boardroom.

You might be thinking the only way to get ahead is to be better than the competition. No doubt being good at what you do is a factor. If you choose to move up the corporate ladder by hoping your competition slips up and you are waiting to prey on their misfortune or error, you have lost your heart. If you withhold information from a colleague because you don't want them to look good, you have lost your heart. When you choose to manipulate the truth to gain a competitive advantage, you have lost your heart. You cannot ever truly be promoted without being of service to others. On the other hand, if you lead with heart and integrity, you are already promoted. A true promotion, instead, comes from wanting everyone else to reach their full potential.

A promotion is not the title you wear on a badge; it's the amount of integrity you own. If you make it to the boardroom without your integrity intact, your foundation will crumble. The energy will be so toxic that an internal battle will ensue. Others will see the truth, and the organization will begin to suffer. You will attempt to remove those that see the truth, but your soul will begin to die.

Newspapers and other media report the names of business leaders that are in trouble because of their lack of integrity. The question we ask here is, "Were they ever really promoted?" They often delude themselves and others by acting as if everything was real when in fact, they were not real at all. While their coffers may appear full, their spiritual bank is empty. They reached the boardroom without any foundation for success.

It's like reading a fictional book and believing it's real. Superman appeared to be genuine, but could he really fly? Superman appeared to be strong, but was he really the man of steel? Once Superman took off his cape, he was no longer Superman. He was never real. Leaders that make it to the boardroom through deception and lies have no costume to fall back on. They were never able to fly. Their authentic self is never realized. They live their life through the ego's ability to create the illusion of power.

Once the mask comes off, you feel a sense of emptiness. You no longer feel powerful, and you start to question whether you belong on the organizational chart because you don't feel real. This is felt the minute you are willing to look in the mirror and accept accountability for your spiritual evolution. You come to realize that you have been hiding behind an illusion, a title without substance, an impostor. Any individual with the ability to see the truth will expose your lack of character. They will shine the light of integrity right on you, and your darkness will be exposed. In the presence of light, darkness disappears.

True power comes from the heart, not from a costume. A true heart is felt by everyone else around the table. If you want to be promoted, just bring love and joy to the lives of others. Sure, you will need to be effective in the execution of the business. You will also bring an energy and enlightenment that will elevate you in the eyes of others. This energy is contagious and infectious. Everyone around you will know that you bring spirit and passion to the workplace, and they will want to share in it. They will know that you are a trusted mentor because everything you do comes from a place of caring. You will not have to spend a lot of time thinking, you can just be yourself.

When you bring your authentic self to the table, that authenticity will transcend throughout the fabric of the organization. Your energy will be so powerful; your peacefulness will be so profound. Your compassion, kindness, and sincerity will inspire others. You will help to bring your organization to the next level—the level of truth. It's from this level that everyone gets promoted. The promotion means that everyone inside of the organization is coming closer to the truth. Integrity becomes more than something found on a vision statement; it is the lifeblood of the organization. Individuals that are full of integrity will be drawn to your doorstep. The darkness will disappear, and true enlightenment will be found everywhere. The spirit will be alive, and an environment will be created for everyone to be their authentic selves.

Kindness, Compassion, Integrity, Service, and Respect: The Path to Continual Promotions

When you lead with kindness, compassion, integrity, service to others, and respect, you have already been promoted. These qualities are like a magnet that draws everyone to you. These are the attributes that are needed in the boardroom and have lasting value. These qualities make being promoted matter. They ensure that your title is in alignment with your spirit, and thus it is "real."

Individuals that possess these qualities lead great organizations. If you embrace these qualities, you will know that whatever you want is already present for you. You will be in the afternoon of your life—meaning and abundance will be yours. It is yours to share with everyone because you are a kind and generous person. The more you share, the more abundance will show up. You will find happiness in everything you do because you bring happiness to others. You don't need to talk about being promoted because you realize that we are all the same. The idea brought forth by a receptionist will be as important to you as an idea brought forth by a manager. You know that we are all equal. The only differentiating factor is whether we choose to live in the morning or afternoon of our lives. Remember, the afternoon of your life is filled with meaning, spirituality, peacefulness, family, and honesty. You will help people to discover their true meaning both spiritually and professionally. They will come to understand that business success is a function of one's spiritual evolution. Every business activity will be rooted in integrity.

It is the ego that leads you to believe that titles and status matter. You might think that having an office makes you more important than being in a cubicle. You might feel that being in the executive suite makes you special. In reality, the size and location of your office is irrelevant. It's not important because it's not real. If having the big office makes you feel better, what will happen if one day it is gone? Are you less of a professional because you work in a cubicle? Don't let your ego convince you that you are superior and more deserving than others. You should always be grateful for what you have and not view the workplace as a competitive playing field. You are not your title. You are not your possessions. You may have more authority, but you are not more powerful than your colleagues. You are you, and that's all that matters.

Bring your energy to a place that makes everyone else around you feel good. Be a positive force. Hold the door open for your assistant. Thank everyone that has been of service to you (and really mean it!). Put your heart into everything you do, and detach from the outcome. You don't control the results; you control your actions and intentions. Make all of your actions and intentions come from a place of integrity. Wish success for others. If you truly want to be promoted, wish for others to be promoted. If you want others to serve you, serve them first. Always seek the best for others, and you will always be guided in a positive direction.

Following these principles, you will never need to worry about the next promotion because you will feel such a sense of inner peace. This feeling is so wonderful that you don't want to change anything. You feel such a sense of accomplishment, a feeling of belonging. When you know that you have made such a difference in other's lives, it's such a great feeling. Your desire to see others happy and content will put pure joy in your heart. Your spirit will be so alive, you will feel pure bliss. Enjoy the moment and know that great things will show up when the time is right!

Remember, leading with and from the heart means you will always be promoted!

Pulse Point 4

Pulse Point 4

Let Light Shine on Your Heart

I love to be in the presence of enlightened leaders possessing true heart. I can feel their kindness and sense of self. They see the light and feel it with total passion. They ignite the light switch of their soul and help others to do the same. Every word they speak and every action they take is from a place of integrity. They are transparent and are glad that you can see their heart. These individuals put everyone at ease. They make everyone around them feel good. When they say "good morning," everyone knows they mean it. When they offer constructive criticism, everyone knows they care about them. When they make a mistake, everyone appreciates that they are human. When they cry, it's because they truly care and are seen as compassionate, not weak.

How do you find true enlightenment? I believe the first step is to recognize whether or not you are operating from a dark place. Darkness exists when you judge others, wish other people harm, are not looking to serve others, and instead expect to be served. This darkness clouds everything you do. Your ego plays tricks on you. You are not being true to yourself and others. You may have found comfort in the darkness, but this comfort is not real. Ultimately, you will come to discover that your life has come up short. You are lost on a dark path. You have missed the light.

You must turn on the light, look in the mirror, and discover the truth. You must stop lying to yourself. Your soul will continue to die if you don't come to terms with who you really are. If you hide behind the mask that conceals the truth, you will whither and die.

Enlightened souls are pure; they don't have to spend a lot of time thinking, they can "just be." They are so connected to their truth, they can simply be themselves. They see the truth in themselves and in every situation that exists. They always feel on solid ground because they have truth on their side. They create their reality with pure ingredients. This purity is from an inner peace based on compassion and integrity. They serve everyone that crosses their path. They want to bring happiness to everyone they meet.

Enlightened people know that giving to others is the path to the light—the soulful light switch. It is through this service that they discover what it means to have a healthy heart. They serve from a place of truth. Every word is pure; every action is kind. Their lives are filled with light.

A heart filled with integrity will keep you on the right path. Your caring and compassion will be embraced by everyone you meet. You will be supported by others because they know you have their best interest at heart. You will not need to look over your shoulder; you will be protected. Enlightened leaders can breathe easy; they don't need to think too much about their actions. They are consistent and have an awareness that signals danger if their actions are in any way not aligned with integrity.

Great leaders help others to find enlightenment. They help others find their own light switch by pushing people to look at their actions with an eye toward positive growth and development. They are truly great mentors. They inspire members of their team to step back and reflect on their actions. It is through this reflection that people learn to reach their optimum potential. They learn to serve others and be kind and peaceful in all of their interactions. They learn to make the transition into the afternoon of their lives with ease. This journey is so wonderful that it forms a special bond with their mentor. This learning carries over into all aspects of their life. They bring joy to their neighbors and add lasting value to our society. They evolve into great mentors and thus perpetuate positive energy for generations to follow.

Inspiration is such a powerful force for our society. Inspired souls bring such joy to our workplace and make our planet such a positive place to live. We need to serve our fellow human beings by inspiring them to reach their full potential. We want them to feel our passion and become inspired by our pure and wonderful energy.

The following are a few reflective questions to see where you are in the journey toward inspiration and enlightenment:

1. Do you know what your purpose in life is?
2. Do you enjoy serving others?
3. Do you view every person as being equal—deserving of total respect?
4. Do you take full accountability for everything you do and say?
5. Are you living a life of true meaning, a life of integrity and spiritual growth?

These questions are intended to make you think. They force you to look in the mirror and reflect. The first question is very important. What is your purpose? This is very different from "what do you do." This is more about why you exist. What is the legacy you wish to leave? Take a few moments to write your obituary. What will you say? Will your obituary speak to your contribution to society or the titles you held? Purpose is more about intention and service to others. It's more about what you give to others than what you give to yourself.

I believe that the most important and inspiring journey is the discovery of one's purpose. Once you find your purpose, you are on a path to inspiration. Living your purpose is like a magnet of pure potential, drawing people to you from a place of joy and enlightenment. You help people to discover their inner strength. You add such positive energy to the planet that peace and fulfillment is felt by everyone who comes into your space. Purposeful leaders are great leaders. They use their purpose toward the service of others. Their purpose connects with their integrity and brings peace to their boardrooms. Their boardrooms are filled with individuals on the journey to lead purposeful lives. When they leave the boardroom, everyone they meet feels positive about their environment.

Many business books talk about helping organizations become "employers of choice." They discuss various strategies such as employee engagement programs and a multitude of employee perks. We ask you to go a step further and realize that these strategies are empty unless they are implemented by leaders who manage from and with their hearts.

Inspirational leaders use their purpose to inspire everyone around them to reach their full potential. Employees feel so alive and so valued that everyone wants to join this organization. They tell all of their friends about what a wonderful environment they work in. The leaders of these organizations are in the afternoon of their lives and understand the true meaning of life. They are helping others to live in the afternoon of their lives as well. It is through this evolution that a work environment feels so vibrant—one you want to be part of and don't want to leave. Why would anyone want to leave a place that is pure, filled with joy, and individually satisfying?

Enlightened environments are places where people discover their true purpose. You are encouraged to think and reflect on the difference you are making for coworkers and customers. It's about value added, not just from a business perspective, but from people's perspective. It's about creating a comfortable environment for spiritual evolution. You learn to treat everyone you meet with total respect. People are kind and compassionate. You are not fulfilled unless you are of service to others.

We must develop boardrooms where enlightened and inspirational leadership are evident. This is a necessary prerequisite to developing business environments that add meaning to our society. These are environments where everyone can feel a sense of pride and fulfillment. The absence of inspiration is equivalent to the absence of heart. We must bring pure inspiration into the boardroom. It is through our service to others that we shine the light of hope.

As we work to revitalize the world economy and strengthen businesses across the globe, we must strive to bring a sense of hope to employees and society as a whole. We must replace fear with hope. We must bring an energy of optimism and a sense of peacefulness that makes everyone feel safe. We do this from a place of kindness and joy. We do this from a place of purpose as enlightened beings that care for our fellow travelers.

Pulse Point 5

Applying the Lessons of the Heart

Application 1: Always Serve Others

*   *Each and every day, evaluate what you can do to serve others.* This may be as simple as holding the door open or helping someone resolve a difficult issue. Your focus and energy must be on helping others, not on expecting them to serve you. The more you serve, the more you will be served.

Application 2: Always Act from a Position of Integrity

*   Are you being authentic with yourself?
*   Are you being authentic with others?
*   Are you doing what you said you would do?
*   Look in the mirror and focus on what you see internally. Focus on what is reflected back.
*   Accept total responsibility for everything you say and do.
*   Engage in win-win scenarios.

- Focus on what needs to be done to achieve positive results. Do not look for opportunities to blame.
- Only change an agreement with the understanding and consensus of others.
- Refrain from making excuses or getting defensive.
- Never execute the messenger.
- Be comfortable saying "I made a mistake."
- Surround yourself with other people whose energy is from a place of high integrity and move away from low-energy people who lack integrity.

Application 3: Always Show Kindness and Compassion

- Always be in a state of gratitude, expressing sincere thanks to anyone and everyone who has helped you.
- Say good morning and good afternoon to everyone you meet, with an energy that is uplifting and heartfelt.
- Listen to and empathize with any person going through a difficult time.
- Send a kind thought to anyone you pass needing support. Remember that even a homeless person deserves the same respect as everyone else.
- Offer sincere praise for everyone deserving recognition.
- View everyone as a whole person and help them find balance and meaning in their lives.
- Help others to improve their performance by offering your assistance. Make sure your message is "I want you to reach your full potential."

Application 4: Always Keep Your Ego in Check

- You are not your title or your possessions. Remember that everyone in the organization is valuable and deserves to be treated equally.
- Be humble; give acknowledgment to others.
- Be willing to give up the fancy office.
- Relinquish the need to be right. Always listen to the opinions of others and place the customer in the middle of the discussion. It does not matter whose idea it was, just concern yourself with getting it right.
- Look in the mirror and ask, "Am I letting my ego get in the way?" If yes, adjust your ego and make a course correction.

Application 5: Always Bring Peace to the Workplace

- You do not need to raise your voice or bang the table to get people's attention. All you need to do is smile, listen, and make your point in a calm and reassuring manner.
- Detach yourself from the outcome. Place your attention and energies on your desired result and accept the outcome without feeling stress or strain. Accept the fact that we only control our actions, not the results of those actions.
- Do not judge anything. Accept everyone and everything as they are. You will feel much more at peace when you let go of the need to judge others as right or wrong.
- Do not give your power away. No one else is responsible for your inner peace but you. If someone is not being peaceful, this must not interrupt your inner feeling of peacefulness.

Application 6: Always Ignite Passion and Purpose

- Discover your purpose and live it every day. Assist others in finding their purpose.
- Be passionate about your work and help others find their passions.
- Inspire others to be creative, allow for mistakes, and do not be judgmental.

Conclusion

W e find ourselves at a crossroads in history. We have been witnessing the erosion of family values. People are working harder and feeling less secure. Many families need to have both parents work in order to make ends meet. People are working eighty-hour workweeks and desperately need to feel a heart in their organizations. They are tired and have a burning desire to feel valued—they want their work to have meaning.

We must do our part as executives and professionals to ensure that the business landscape is filled with heart. My hope is that all current and future leaders will embrace the principles outlined in this book with the same enthusiasm and commitment that they watch their quarterly results being applauded by Wall Street. My hope is that we create a shift in corporate thinking that will motivate current and future generations of business leaders to not only bring peace to their workplace, but also contribute to creating peace in the world.

We must all come together around a common cause—to make this world a better place to live and work. We must make our businesses better places for our employees to grow and thus for our organizations and our careers to prosper well into the future.

I thank you for your support and willingness to take your heart and soul into the boardroom!

Appendix

A True Story of Heart and Soul in the Boardroom

The following is a true story about a leader named Warren, a man who made it to the boardroom with his heart totally intact. I had the privilege of working for Warren many years ago at an international manufacturing company.

Warren was one of the kindest and most compassionate leaders I had ever worked for. He was in charge of the Distribution Division. He was responsible for ensuring that the supply chain ran effectively in servicing accounts throughout the United States.

When something went wrong, Warren was on the hot seat. He always assumed full responsibility for anything that did not go according to plan, never blaming anyone else. When I made a mistake, Warren coached me to be successful the next time. He was always respectful, complimenting me in public, offering constructive criticism in private.

I remember the day I received a call telling me that my grandmother had suffered a heart attack and was taken to the hospital. Warren told me to leave immediately and not worry about my work. He called me that evening to see how my grandmother and I were doing.

I recall the day Warren encouraged me to develop course materials and provide training support for a new distribution program called DRP.

What I remember most was the confidence he had in me. I knew that he would support me to ensure that I would be successful. One day, the president said to Warren, "Congratulations, Warren, on the excellent job you did in providing the DRP staff training." Warren replied, "You have Bob to thank, not me." I recall the look on the president's face. He just smiled. To this day, I truly believe that smile was acknowledgment of the strength of Warren's character.

The president often conferred with Warren. He respected Warren and knew that if he wanted the truth, Warren was the leader to seek out. Everyone knew who Warren was because he was a man of very high integrity.

Warren was a great talent scout. He surrounded himself with people who displayed high integrity and always went out of his way to serve others. Every morning, Warren would walk through the hallways saying good morning to his team and anyone else he met along the way. He treated the receptionist with the same respect as the president. Warren was always interested in your suggestions and gave every idea fair consideration. He thanked you for your input, making you want to try even harder.

Warren's division had the lowest turnover rate in the company and the highest productivity. We not only respected Warren; we loved him. He was a great leader and a wonderful human being.

If Warren went to the cafeteria, he always asked if he could bring you back a cup of coffee, and he really meant it!

Warren proved the point and the premise of the book—you can be highly effective in the executive role by leading with a heart. When you do, the organization is more profitable. The employees are more committed and happier, and ultimately, the world is a better place.

I miss you, Warren; thanks for the memories. You were, and are, a man of true heart—a man that brought your heart and soul to the boardroom every day.

Testimonials

Testimonials

"What distinguishes the truly great organizations from those that are mediocre? It's integrity, heart, compassion, and truly caring about your employees. Bob Cooper's book is a manual for how every business should conduct itself. We hear time and time again that one must be tough and ruthless to get ahead in the marketplace. People who believe that fail to realize the value their employees provide. Employees who work in a difficult environment will not produce to their highest capabilities. Treating employees right leads to a better business model, one where profits are maximized. Bob puts it very well when he says, 'Compassion + Integrity = Profits.' I firmly believe that *Heart and Soul in the Boardroom* is a roadmap to business success."

—John Fontana
President
The Fontana Group

"*Heart and Soul in the Boardroom* is written 'from the heart,' 'for the heart.' It reawakens the reader's understanding that people are the greatest resource in any business and, as such, need to be encouraged, allowed, and even empowered to expand to their fullest potential. This is accomplished by infusing the workplace with 'heartfelt' qualities such as respect, appreciation, and most importantly, integrity. The business culture that made America great has all but disappeared. The current culture and generation of business executives are rarely leading from their hearts. The results are evident—corporations are in crisis. Open heart surgery is vitally important in our boardrooms. If we are to restore stability and profitability in world markets, there must be a new mindset—one that comes from the heart. *Heart and Soul in the Boardroom* is a must read for both business students and executives alike."

—Peter Lorenzo, MS, RPh
Director, Medical Department
Joint Industry Board of the Electrical Industry

Index

A

authenticity, 10, 25

C

compassion, 18–21, 24–26, 30, 36

E

ego, 13, 15, 24, 27, 29, 37
"employers of choice," 32
enlightened people, 14, 23

H

heart, 11–15, 17–21, 23, 25, 27, 30

I

inspiration, 7, 31–32
integrity, 7, 9, 12, 14, 18–22, 24–27,
    29–31, 35–36, 42–44
    absence of, 20

K

kindness, 12–13, 19–21, 25–26, 29,
    33, 36

L

leaders
    enlightened, 29–30
    inspirational, 32

without hearts, 12, 25, 30–31
Lessons of the Heart, 36–37
life stages
  afternoon, 14, 30, 32
  morning, 9, 14–15, 26, 42

P

peace, 15, 19, 21, 31–32, 37, 39
profitability, 17–18, 21, 44
  formulas for producing, 17–18
promotion
  false, 23
  true, 24
    path to, 26
purpose, 31–33, 38

S

self-respect, 13
service, 13, 24, 26–27, 30–32
  law of, 15
sincerity, 15, 25
spiritual evolution, 25–26
success
  business, 26
  true meaning of, 21

T

truth, 12–14, 19–21, 23–25, 30, 42

W

Warren (leader with a heart), 41–42
work environments, enlightened, 32

www.ingramcontent.com/pod-product-compliance
Lightning Source LLC
Chambersburg PA
CBHW021938170526
45157CB00005B/2338